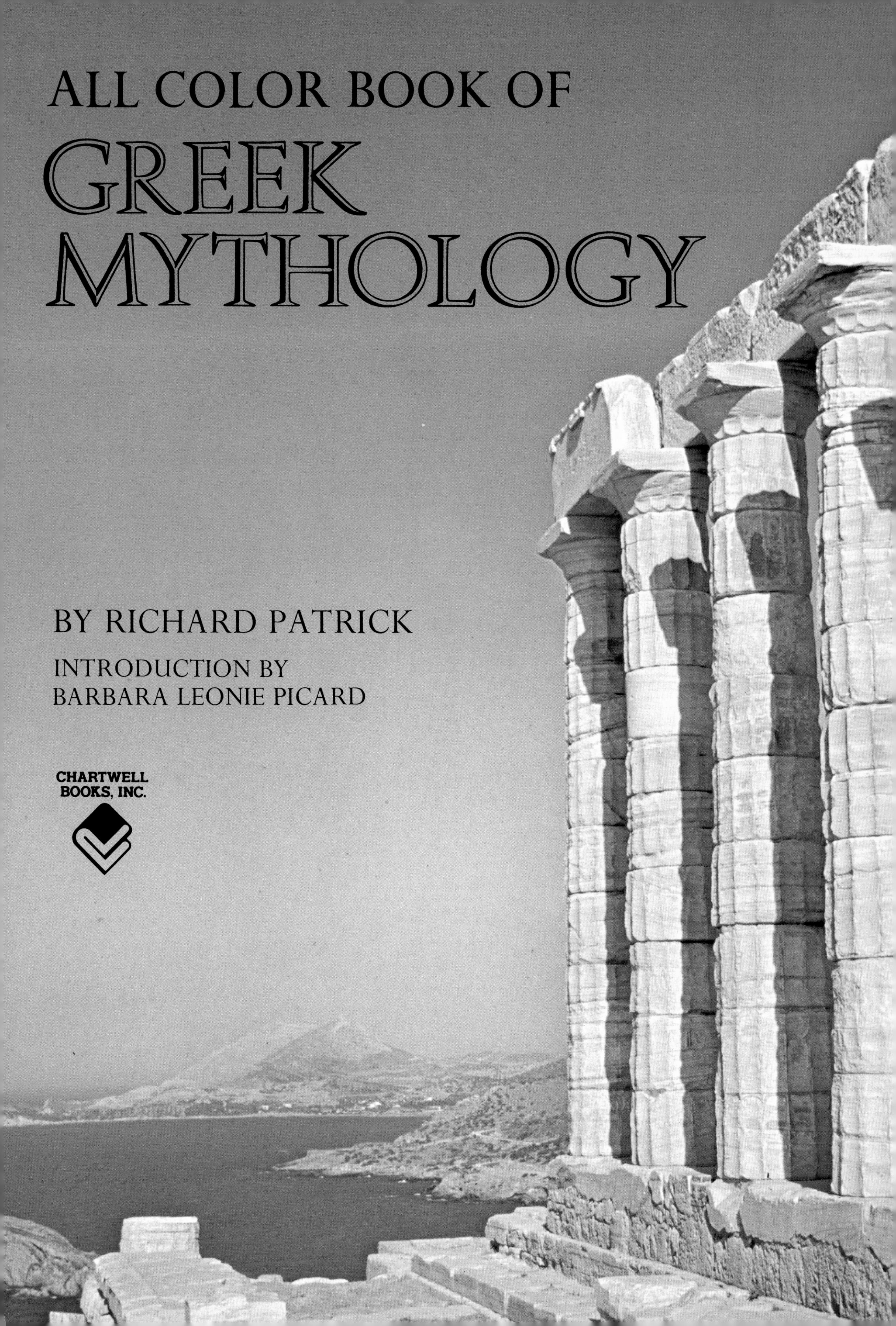

ALL COLOR BOOK OF GREEK MYTHOLOGY

BY RICHARD PATRICK

INTRODUCTION BY
BARBARA LEONIE PICARD

CHARTWELL
BOOKS, INC.

This 1989 edition
published by
Chartwell Books, Inc.
A Division of Book Sales Inc.
110 Enterprise Avenue
Secaucus
New Jersey 07094

ISBN 1-55521-359-6

Produced by Mandarin Offset
Printed in Hong Kong

II
THE COMING OF ORDER

10

Plate 10

Little is known for certain about the gods of the Greeks in the dark centuries that followed the destruction of the Minoan culture. The Indo-European migrations were bringing new men down into the peninsula in the early part of the second millennium and a new, male-orientated society was mingling with the old. The Achaeans—those described by Homer—came in the thirteenth century BC; they were warlike and ruthless and the tide seemed to be irreversible. A god-king challenged the Mother. Tradition, however, dies hard, and the new All-powerful was given a childhood in Crete. The picture shows the cave of Dicte, on the Aegean Hill, where Rhea, the mother of Zeus, hid her son from his father Cronus.

11

12

13

Plate 11

The shaft graves at Mycenae. Towards the end of the second millennium the Achaeans were followed by the Dorians; a usurper race was in fact displaced by one even more powerful though adhering to much the same religious ideas. Sky-gods replaced the Mother in all parts of Greece, a process often brought about by the taking of wives from the old ruling clans, and imposing a new religion together with a new order. But it was by no means a peaceful process; and the troubled world to which the Homeric heroes returned after the fall of Troy is probably a reflection of this.

Plate 12

The castration of Uranus. The stories of the gods and their beginnings were given a definite shape by Homer and Hesiod, and were generally accepted by the eighth and seventh centuries BC. Ge, or Mother Earth, emerged from Chaos and bore Uranus, the starry universe, who became her consort. All their children were hated by Uranus who feared any challenge to his rule, and the Titans, the Giants, the Cyclops and Cronus were confined to the nether world. The angry Earth Mother released her youngest son, Cronus, and encouraged him to castrate his father and rule in his place.

Plate 13

The peak of Mount Olympus. When Cronus succeeded to his father's place he took his sister Rhea as his consort. (Interestingly, Rhea was probably the name by which the Mother was known in Crete.) Warned by Ge that one of his children would destroy him, he followed his father and swallowed his children as soon as they were born. The enraged Rhea gave him a stone to swallow in place of his third son, Zeus, whom she hid until he reached manhood. Zeus then enlisted the help of Cyclops, Giants, some of the Titans (including Prometheus) and waged war on Cronus and the rest of the Titans from Mount Olympus. Zeus was victorious; Cronus disappeared from myth and the stage was set for the ordering of the gods and their place in the consciousness of the Greeks. Even Zeus was insecure to begin with though he was eventually to rule unchallenged.

Plate 14

The great archaeologist Schliemann undertook the excavation of Mycenae which was the seat of the High King Agamemnon and the gold mask is from one of the royal graves. When Schliemann lifted it he saw for a brief moment the face of a fair-bearded king, before it crumbled to dust. He sent a telegram to the King of Greece: 'I have gazed upon the face of Agamemnon.' It is certain now that the fair-bearded king will never be identified and there is no way of ascertaining who he was. But the intense drama of that moment in the grave is easy to imagine.

III
THE OLYMPIANS

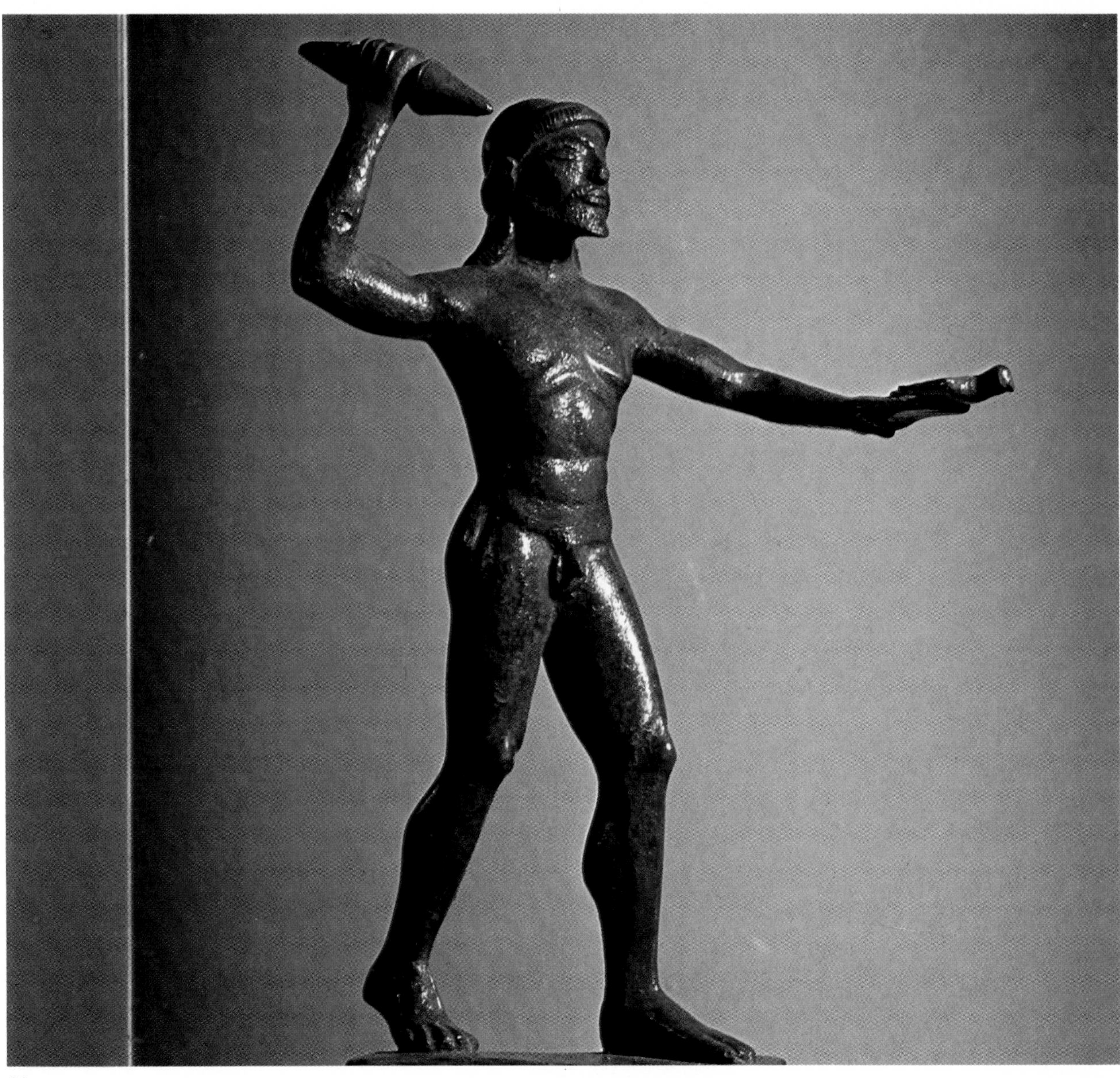

19

Plate 19

A Greek bronze of Zeus bearing a thunderbolt. As the sky god he is the embodiment of an idea which was ancient long before the Dorians found their way down into Greece, and can be definitely identified in the religion of ancient India. He was originally the Indo-European *weather* god as well—he who controlled the thunder and the rain, a deity of the first importance to migratory herdsmen. The third son of Cronus according to Hesiod, he is made the first son by Homer, who also describes the division of the world among the three sons: Poseidon was given the seas and Hades the underworld; Zeus himself retained the heavens. He ruled by the counsel of Ge—through all the changes in Greek religion the Mother remained. She could both foretell the future and act as the instrument of fate. The bronze is fifth-century and comes from Dodona, where there was an oracle of Zeus.

20

Plate 20

The most famous temple of Zeus in classical Greece was the one at Olympia—not, as might be supposed, somewhere near Mount Olympus; Olympia was in Elis, in the Peloponnese. The Olympic Games were held there, every fourth year, and in the sacred precinct were two temples, one to Hera and a magnificent one to Zeus. It was 220 feet long and 90 feet wide; the columns were 30 feet high. Next to Delphi Olympia was the greatest religious centre of Greece. It retained its position until the fourth century AD, when the Emperor Theodosius, a Christian, issued an edict enjoining the destruction of all pagan sites.

Plate 21

Zeus enthroned. This impressive marble statue shows him as ruler and father. He was the dispenser of good and evil in the fortunes of men, and the giver of laws that ruled the course of events. He had many titles: defender of the house, defender of the hearth, upholder of the right to liberty, maintainer of the laws of hospitality, guardian of property. He was also *Chthonios*, the god of the earth and the giver of fertility, a title which showed the persistence of the connection in Greek minds of the male god as a consort. Despite the extraordinary virtues which were uttered in his praise Zeus was, paradoxically, a very human god. His rages were accepted as natural bad temper and his casual disregard of marriage laws no obstacle to an acceptance of him as both lawgiver and *paterfamilias*. His love affairs with members of both sexes were the subject of comedy and his treatment of Prometheus seen as a regrettable stage in the establishment of order.

Plate 22

The marriage of Zeus and Hera, from the fifth-century temple at Selinunte. Hera was one of the children of Cronus and Rhea and thus sister as well as wife to Zeus. Her character in Greek mythology is not attractive and her moments of angry spite were almost always caused through jealousy of her husband's amours. Certainly he was wayward enough to test the most patient wife but the many stories of his infidelities can be traced to something more than mere lustfulness. The ascendancy of the god, as opposed to the goddess with whom the native Greeks had been familiar for centuries, was often accomplished by the union of a local deity with the newcomer —and the object of his lust can often be identified in this way. Since many royal houses claimed descent from him his extra-marital adventures were also required to cover a very wide field.

22

Plate 23

One of the loves of Zeus was Europa, the daughter of Agenor, King of Tyre. She used to walk with her companions near the seashore, and one day she noticed a beautiful white bull among her father's cattle. She hung garlands on his horns and then climbed on his back—whereupon the bull plunged into the sea and swam away with her. He carried her to the island of Crete and took his pleasure of her there, and the children of this union were Minos, Rhadamanthus and Sarpedon. The reigning king of Crete, Asterius, married Europa and having no sons of his own adopted hers. The connections with Crete in the myth is interesting as it raises the factor of the bull cult. Europa is seen here on a sixth-century vase painting from Caere.

23

24

Plate 24

Zeus in the guise of a swan pays court to Leda—an affair which was to have serious consequences. She was the daughter of Thestios, King of Aetolia and the wife of Tyndareus, King of Sparta. Leda liked to bathe in the river Eurotas, where one day she saw a swan swimming beside her. The swan being Zeus, the sequel was inevitable— though Leda must have been rather disconcerted to find herself laying eggs as the result of her dalliance. However, Tyndareus lay with her that night too and there is no record in the myths that he found his wife's way of bearing children unusual. Three children emerged from the egg: Castor and Pollux, and the beautiful Helen.

25

26

Plate 25

The story of Leda and the swan may have arisen from a memory of a nature cult; they were familiar in Greece and Crete in early times. This gold pendant is from Aegina but the workmanship is Cretan. A god or a priest is standing on a lotus plant, holding a swan in each hand. *c* 2,000 BC.

Plate 26

Hera was the legitimate consort of Zeus and occupied first place among the goddesses of the Greeks. Homer describes her as 'Argive' Hera, a reference to the origin of her cult in Argos. Her character was formidable and there is good reason to see her as the survival of a powerful cult of the Mother in Argos—marrying her was perhaps the only way open to Zeus of reconciling his power with hers: that is to say that the new Greeks found this way of reconciling the original people with themselves; Hera, as Mother, would have had no consort at all or else one of little importance. The patron and guardian of marriage, Hera also watched over women in childbirth and her blessing was sought to bring fruitfulness to the womb. She makes a striking appearance in the myth of the Argonauts as the befriender of Jason against his enemy Pelias; Pelias had withheld his homage to the goddess—a dangerous thing to do where Hera was concerned. In this Attic red-figured vase she is seen with Hebe, her daughter by Zeus who was cup-bearer to the gods.

Plate 27

Hera's temple at Agrigento, the ancient Acragas. Acragas was on the south-west coast of Sicily, an island popular with emigrant Greeks throughout their history. The city prospered through its trade with Carthage and built superb temples in the classical style; the poet Pindar in particular was lavish in his praise. The city, which was founded in the sixth century BC, was sacked by the Carthaginians during one of their conflicts with Rome in 405.

28

Plate 28

Hera gives the charge of the winds to Aeolus. Zeus himself found the winds a troublesome responsibility; they might, when his attention was diverted, have blown both earth and sea away. He confined them within a cliff that floated in the Tyrrhenian Sea among some islands, and to those islands Aeolus sailed in search of a home. That the bestowal of the winds on Aeolus should have been the action of Hera is explained by one authority in terms of Hera's original character as the Mother: the winds were her messengers. Delacroix's painting is distinctly Romantic in tone but the figure of Aeolus, after whom the Aeolian islands were named, has the appropriate heroic look.

29

Plate 29

Poseidon, the brother of Zeus and the lord of the seas. He was also, and probably more significantly, the god chiefly connected with horses, which suggests that his origin was very ancient indeed and dated from the time of the migrations. (The importance of the sea to the Greeks came much later.) The horse was a creature of enormous importance to the Indo-European migrants; it provided transport, food, clothing and was a visible symbol of fertility. Poseidon's title, *Hippios,* identifies him firmly and the horse appears again and again in the traditions of the Greeks.
When Greek religion was formalized the ancient deity was probably given the domain that seemed closest to his original character, following the ancient idea that river (water) gods were horses and the symbolism of the white crests of the waves. Poseidon was not, apparently, content with his portion; he squabbled with Athene for the possession of Attica and with Hera for that of Aegina.

Plate 30

A marble group from Smyrna, dating from the second century AD. The sculpture is notable not only for its late date but also because it actually shows Poseidon and Demeter together. The myth concerning them is very strange and probably a confusion of several different stories. Poseidon lusted after Demeter (his sister according to Hesiod) but she would have none of him, grieving as she was over her lost daughter Persephone. To escape his attentions Demeter turned herself into a mare, and slipped in among the horse herds of Arcadia. However her transformation had not escaped the keen eye of Poseidon; he promptly turned himself into a stallion and joined the herd too. The furious Demeter soon found herself mounted by a triumphant Poseidon. The offspring of this remarkable coupling was the magical horse, Arion, who became the property of Adrastus, King of Argos.

30

Plate 31

Poseidon's temple on the promontory at Sounion, the cape which forms the southern tip of Attica. The cape was a welcome landmark for the Athenian sailors making for the Piraeus and there was a temple to Poseidon under construction which was destroyed by the Persians before it could be completed. The columns which survive are from the marble temple to the god of the seas built by the Athenians in the late fifth century BC. It was at Cape Sounion that Apollo struck down Menelaus' pilot on the voyage back from Sparta. Menelaus was delayed and his brother Agamemnon, returning alone to Mycenae, fell victim to Clytemnestra and Aegisthus.

31

Plate 32

Demeter, the goddess who more than any other personified for the Greeks the timeless idea of the fruitful earth. She was an ancient deity of mainland Greece, the corn-goddess on whom survival depended. In later times she is also the sorrowing mother of Persephone who was abducted by Hades, the god of the underworld. Her anguished search for her daughter led her to neglect the earth and it ceased to be fruitful: Zeus had to intervene lest the earth became completely barren and mankind perished. She was at Eleusis when her daughter was restored to her, and the Mysteries of her cult were celebrated there: those and the great festival of the Thesmophoria (of Demeter Thesmophoros—the bringer of treasures) were the most popular and widely attended of all Greek religion. Demeter as the sorrowing mother is strikingly portrayed in this marble of the fourth century BC.

32

33

Plate 33

Demeter and Kore. This vase painting shows mother and daughter (*kore*—maiden) with ears of corn. 'The maiden' was another way of referring to Persephone and this lends weight to the opinion that she was simply another aspect of the same goddess. The ancient Mother was in some respects the eternal woman—the mother who bore the maiden, who became a mother, who later attended on other births, who laid out the dead, who died herself, who was renewed as the maiden, who became a mother. . . . The myth relates how Persephone, at the intervention of Zeus, would have been permanently returned by Hades; but she had eaten the food of the dead—four pomegranate seeds—and was really bound to Hades for ever. In the end the god of the underworld exacted a price for her release: for each of the seeds she ate she would have to spend a month with him. This was agreed: each year Persephone returns to Hades, and winter falls upon the land.

34

Plate 34

Hades, seen with Persephone on a Greek amphora found in Apulia. He was the brother of Zeus, Poseidon, and Demeter also; Hesiod's arrangement of the family of the Olympians makes him a lustful uncle. To the Greeks he was the ruler of the world of the dead and they also gave this name to his realm, which was separated from the world of the living by the river Styx. The dead were ferried across by Charon, whose fee for the service was placed in the mouth of the corpse. The burial rites were therefore all-important. At the entrance to Hades stood the watch-dog Cerberus, who prevented those who entered from ever leaving again. Hades helped in the defeat of Cronus by stealing his weapons, and while not regarded with affection by the Greeks he exacted a great deal of respect. But he was not a *punisher*—the Greeks had no conception of any god who might be equated with Satan.

35

Plate 35

The association of Persephone and Hades is probably a strand of the ancient veneration of the Mother as the bestower of all things and she to whom all departed when life had run its course. Not surprisingly this aspect of the Mother was rarely expressed but the Maiden and Mother partners were often to be seen in votive figures and works of art. This sixth-century terracotta shows them as identical. It comes from Corinth and is now in the British Museum.

Plate 36

Triptolemos was the son of the King of Eleusis who offered kindness to the exhausted Demeter after her wanderings. He alone recognized the goddess and it was he who told her that her daughter was in the possession of Hades. When Demeter was reunited with Persephone she rewarded Triptolemos with the knowledge of agriculture, and through him initiated the Mysteries at Eleusis. He was thereafter regarded as a culture hero; the spread of agriculture as the basis for an ordered and increasingly civilized life was attributed to him, and he was honoured at the Mysteries and at the Thesmophoria. He is seen here as a boy, receiving from Demeter the first sprig of corn. Bas-relief of the fifth century BC, now in the National Museum, Athens.

36

Plate 37

The ruins of the fifth-century temple of Demeter at Paestum. Paestum, which lies on the coast below Naples, was founded by Greek colonists in 600 BC. It flourished for centuries and was a wealthy city, as the impressive ruins testify; but the encroaching marshes made it unhealthy and it was gradually deserted during the Roman Empire.

37

38

39

Plate 38

The Acropolis, seen from the Philopappus Hill. The word means 'upper city' and an eminence was commonly chosen in ancient times to give the city itself a citadel. The flat rock is 200 feet higher than Athens and, fittingly, it was the setting for the most famous temple ever built—the Parthenon, the temple of Athene Parthenos or Athene the Maiden. She was the patron goddess of Athens; the myth tells of the rivalry for the possession of Attica, and how Poseidon disputed Athene's claim. A council of the gods declared that the victor should be the one who gave to man the greatest gift. Poseidon struck the ground with his trident, and created the first horse. But Athene planted an olive tree and she was adjudged the victor. The meaning of the myth is plain: it is generally agreed by scholars that the figure of Athene goes back to archaic times, long before the Greeks arrived in the peninsula.

Plate 39

Athene was the daughter of Zeus and Metis—an unwilling Metis who did her best to escape the god's attentions. Ge (Mother Earth) warned Zeus that the child of this union would be a girl but if he persisted in his attentions and she conceived a second child it would be a son, and depose him just as he had deposed his father Cronus. Zeus took no chances with any child of Metis: as soon as he could get close enough to her he swallowed her whole. In due course he began to feel violent headaches, which increased in severity so that his howling began to shake the heavens. Hermes divined the cause of discomfort; he fetched Hephaestos, who split Zeus' skull open. Athene sprang forth with a great shout, fully armed.

40

Plate 40

The Parthenon, constructed during the age of Pericles between 447 and 438 BC. It was built entirely of Pentelic marble and its perfect proportions combine strength and grace; it is the Doric style at the peak of perfection. The lovely temple to Athene was revered for nearly a thousand years; then the Byzantines gutted the interior to make it a Christian church. This barbarism was furthered by the Franks in the thirteenth century AD, by the Turks in the fifteenth, and by the Venetians in the seventeenth century, so the Parthenon was a ruin when Lord Elgin removed the sculptures in the nineteenth. Many of them are in the British Museum.

Plate 41

Apollo, as the Etruscans saw him. A terracotta statue of the fifth century BC from Veii depicts a rather sinister god. Apollo was the son of Zeus and Leto, daughter of the Titans Coeus and Phoebe. Leto was the victim of Hera's jealousy, and for fear of the goddess's wrath no land would receive Leto when her time drew near. She made her way to Ortygia near Delos; the two islands floated in the sea, and only became anchored after Leto's children were delivered. First she gave birth to a girl, Artemis, who was no sooner born than she helped her mother cross to Delos. Apollo was born there on the north side of Mount Cynthus and was a favoured child from the beginning: Themis fed him on nectar and ambrosia, and Hephaestos brought him arms when he was only four days old. Apollo was a late-comer among the gods of Greece, and probably had his origins among the migrating peoples. But the conception of a golden son, just and beautiful and a benefactor, is a popular one and his counterpart can be found in many mythologies.

41

42

43

Plate 42

Mount Parnassus in the spring, still crowned by the winter snows. When he left Delos Apollo went in search of the serpent Python, who had at Hera's orders tormented Leto in her wanderings. He found him on Parnassus and wounded him with arrows; but Python managed to escape and fled to the oracle of Mother Earth at Delphi. Apollo dared to follow him into the sacred place where he killed him by the chasm from where the oracular utterances came.

Plate 43

Delphi lies on the south-west spur of Mount Parnassus and was an oracular shrine in the time before the Olympians, and the Greeks wisely chose to maintain its reputation. When Apollo killed Python there he was required to undergo purification for defilining a holy place; but he coaxed the art of prophecy from the god Pan (significantly, Pan was a nature god as old as the Mother herself) and then returned to Delphi. He seized the shrine for himself and Delphi became the most venerated site in Greece, the object of endless pilgrimages where the priests of Apollo sat on a tripod over the sacred chasm giving the answers to the questions of suppliants. The Delphic Oracle was the supreme authority on matters of religion. Only two other gods were represented at Delphi, Dionysus and Athene. The picture shows the Tholos, one of the buildings in the precinct dedicated to Athene. It dates from the fourth century BC.

Plate 44

Apollo with his lyre, pouring a libation. He was the god of light (Phoebus, the bright), youth, prophecy and music—especially of the lyre. His other charge, the care of flocks and herds, points to his origin among the Indo-European migrants. Apollo's companions as the god of music—and of most the arts—were Dionysus as the patron of the theatre, and the Muses, the daughters of Zeus by Mnemosyne (memory). Apollo was a dangerous god to be involved with—King Midas was given asses' ears and Marsyas the satyr was flayed alive when they both doubted Apollo's musical supremacy—and it thus seems strange that the Greeks seemed to associate him with moral excellence. His cult in Delphi had an enormous influence in the extension of tolerance; it prescribed expiation for all crimes and actively discouraged the ancient idea of vengeance. But the Delphic Apollo is the later personification; the ancient god may well have been one to fear. The illustration is from a Greek dish of the fifth century BC, now in the museum at Delphi.

44

45

Plate 45

A relief of the first century BC showing a Muse playing a lyre. When the gods defeated the Titans Zeus was asked to create divinities capable of celebrating the victory. He lay with Mnmosyne for nine nights and the nine daughters of this union were the Muses. Though their preferred home was Mount Helicon they liked to visit Parnassus where they sought the waters of the Castalian spring and where they enjoyed the company of Apollo. The waters of the spring were used in purification rites in the temple at Delphi and were also given to the Pythoness (priestess) of the oracle to drink.

46

47

Plate 46

An early Greek terracotta, probably a votive offering, which represents the goddess Artemis. Homer describes Artemis as Mistress of Beasts and the description was as true of the goddess the Greeks venerated as it was of the Mother of whom she is another aspect. Like her twin brother Apollo she bore a name which was not Greek in origin but unlike him she was an original deity of Greece and the Aegean. Her origins, like those of so many Greek gods, clung to her even when she was transformed into an Olympian; thus she is a virgin goddess while at the same time a giver of fertility, and her domain is the wild earth, the forests and hills where she hunts. Again, her pleading with Asklepios to restore life to the dead Hippolytus suggests a very human and womanly love. In the tragedy by Euripides Hippolytus was presented as a man of perfect purity—a fit companion for Artemis. Possibly their story is a survival of the goddess's original character; as an aspect of the Mother she would have had a consort. The terracotta shown here portrays the Mistress of Beasts carrying a small unidentifiable animal, possibly a fawn. Small animals were sacrified to her at her annual festival at Patrae.

Plate 47

Much more in keeping with the character of the Mother from whom she stemmed is the Artemis of Ephesus, the Ionian city which in classical times was a great seaport and the rival of Antioch and Alexandria. The cult of Artemis the giver of fertility had an ancient centre near the city and it was there that King Croesus ordered the building of a temple to her, a building which was to become one of the wonders of the ancient world. It was from Ephesus, not from Greece, that the cult of the goddess found its way to Rome. There, as Diana, she exacted the same confusion of venerations that she enjoyed in Greece. The city of Ephesus eventually declined; the silt of the Cayster river choked the harbour and now the remains of her glory lie several miles inland.

Plate 48

The virgin huntress. In this manifestation Artemis appears in the *Iliad*—and cuts rather a poor figure. She tries conclusions with the other Olympians present at the siege of Troy (the gods took definite sides in the struggle) and arouses the wrath of Hera, who tells her scornfully that the killing of animals is her proper place. However, if she *will* challenge her betters she must suffer the consequences: Hera then seizes Artemis' wrists in one hand and grabs her quiver and arrows with the other; she beats her victim about the head with them until the hapless Artemis breaks free and flies weeping to Olympus to be comforted by her father Zeus. Nevertheless Artemis was a firm favourite with women, especially those in the humbler walks of life who probably knew her best in her original form.

49

Plate 49

Hephaestos, the divine artificer and god of fire was the maker of magical things for gods and men, such as the armour of Achilles and Agamemnon's sceptre. The son of Zeus and Hera, he was such a sickly child at birth that Hera in disgust flung him from Olympus. He fell into the sea where Thetis (the mother of Achilles) and Eurynome found and cared for him, giving him a forge to work in. He made such exquisite jewellery that it attracted the attention of his cold-hearted mother and she had her son brought back to Olympus to take his proper place. Later he intervened in a quarrel between Hera and Zeus who hurled him from Olympus again. He returned to Olympus permanently lamed, but the strength of Hephaestos was in his mighty arms and shoulders which most metal workers develop. His cult centres were always to be found in the cities, where the craft was most intensely practised.

Plate 50

Boucher's painting *The Forges of Vulcan* is based on later accretions; the god is in fact Hephaestos and he is shown here with Aphrodite. The painting suggests domestic harmony; but the marriage was ordered by Zeus and Aphrodite resented being married off to the lame, ungainly smith god. Her lover was Ares, the war god, and the furious Hephaestos constructed an invisible net of bronze to cover the bed, and trapped the guilty pair by pretending to be absent. He then had his revenge when the rest of the Olympians gathered round to laugh at Ares and Aphrodite in their public humiliation.

50

Plate 51

The temple of Hephaestos in Athens, north-west of the Acropolis. Traditionally called the Theseum, this well-preserved small temple was mis-named, probably because some of the sculptures relate to the adventures of Theseus. It is now generally agreed that it was in fact a shrine to Hephaestos.

51

Plate 52

Aphrodite, the goddess of love. Homer and Hesiod differed in their account of her origins; Hesiod said that she arose from the sea foam which gathered around the genitals of Uranus when Cronus cast them down; Homer makes her the daughter of Zeus and Dione, and therefore a respectable member of the Olympian pantheon. She was in fact an ancient goddess of the eastern Mediterranean and can be equated with the Asian goddess Astarte. This marble statue from the Rhodes Museum shows her shaking out her hair after emerging from the waves. She was worshipped in Greece in two different manifestations, Aphrodite Urania (the higher, purer love) and Aphrodite Pandemos (sensual lust). Her worship was generally austere but it is interesting to note that prostitutes regarded her as their patron, and that there was a sacred prostitution in her cult at Corinth.

52

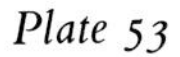

Plate 53

Dionysus returns to Greece to claim his place among the gods. To the north of Greece, in Thrace and Macedonia, there was in ancient times a powerful cult of the spirit of nature and fertility that expressed itself in orgiastic rites, human sacrifice and animal worship. This found its way to Greece around 1,000 BC and its ecstatic character made an irresistible appeal. At the centre of the cult was Dionysus, who came to represent the forces of life and nature in animals and the fruits of the growing plants; eventually he was regarded as the god of wine. But in earlier times there was no need for his followers—mostly women—to drink; their frenzies were self induced, and so uncontrollable that it was dangerous to encounter a band of women in a Dionysiac frenzy. Animals, and sometimes children, were torn to pieces and eaten—the belief existing that to devour a part of an animal was to partake of the god himself, a true sacramental meal.

53

54

Plate 54

An Etruscan terracotta showing the head of a satyr. The spirits of wild life, satyrs were bestial in both their desires and their behaviour and were often pictured with animal characteristics—those of a horse or a goat—to emphasize their connection with fertility. They were attendants on Dionysus, and some myths describe them as taking part in the tutoring of the young god.

55

Plate 55

An Etruscan bronze of the fifth century BC showing a satyr and a maenad. The maenads were votaries of Dionysus—the word means 'mad women', a description of their behaviour during their frenzied worship. In the play by Euripides, *The Bacchae*, the cult of Dionysus is resisted by Pentheus, King of Thebes, and his mother Agave. Dionysus rouses the women of Thebes to a frenzy and sends them to take part in his rites on the mountainside; then the god reappears in the guise of a votary and persuades the king to spy on them, inducing the same frenzy in Agave that affects the other women. The hapless Pentheus is torn to pieces by the maenads, and Agave returns to the palace carrying a head she has torn from a man's shoulders. Only when her frenzy abates does she realize that the head is her son's. Followers of the god were also called *bakchoi*, and the name Bacchus was the Latin one used by the Romans for their version of Dionysus.

Plate 56

The theatre at Delphi. Dionysus was made respectable by Hesiod, and joined the Olympians as the son of Zeus and Semele. Apollo is credited with the 'taming' of the wilder excesses of Dionysiac religion. During the older, more bestial orgies the maenads often wore masks, and the god was represented by a mask on a pole; the pole was draped with an animal skin but the mask was always human, and this aspect of the cult was the beginning of drama as an art. Apollo admitted Dionysus to his side at Delphi—in other words the powerful cult was admitted to the gentler forms of state religion. By the fifth century BC dramatic festivals were an integral part of Greek culture; one of the most noteworthy festivals was the great Dionysia—the spring festival of Dionysus.

63

Plate 63

The theatre at Epidauros, the Greek city which owed its fame to Asklepios—the centre of his cult was here. Patients would visit the temple and sleep there; a cure would sometimes be communicated through dreams, sometimes be effected during sleep. Snakes were kept in the temple and regarded as sacred, the snake being the god's emblem, and when new cult centres were founded young serpents were taken there from Epidauros. (The small yellow snakes to be seen in the region today, harmless creatures, are very likely those described by the ancient Greek traveller Pausanias). The theatre dates from the fourth century BC and is one of the most perfect of its kind. It is in regular use today.

64

Plate 64

The great god Pan depicted in bronze by an Etruscan sculptor of the fourth century BC. A very ancient god indeed, his cult was in Arcadia where Mount Maenalus was sacred to him. A herdsman's god, he came to be associated with goats which were the principal livestock of that part of Greece. In Homer he is made the son of Hermes who was an Olympian and also, originally, a god of Arcadia. The cult of Pan reached beyond his native pastures and by the fifth century BC he had a cave shrine on the Acropolis. He was reputed to be the cause of sudden and groundless fear—panic fear—that could overcome people in desolate, lonely places, and his principal diversion, sex, was the natural outcome of his connection with the fertility of flocks. Though a minor god in classical Greece, Pan enjoyed a healthy respect. It was from him that Apollo learned the art of prophecy.

65

Plate 65

An Etruscan terracotta relief from Cerveteri showing a satyr dancing with a maenad. Satyrs were originally shown with some animal-like features, those of a horse or a goat, and were variously called the brothers of the nymphs or the spirits of the wild countryside. They were associated with both Dionysus and Pan and in later Greek art often depicted as the familiars of Dionysus in his character of god of wine. As the familiars of Pan they often wore horns and walked on hoofs and this association, particularly, was the one that gave them in later centuries their identification as the male symbols of sexuality. The satyr shown here seems little more than a frisky young man; but in Roman art that is how he frequently appears.

66

Plate 66

A Lycian sarcophagus of the fourth century BC, showing two centaurs in combat on the front panel. These strange creatures were originally depicted as horses with the head of a man. The later, more familiar idea of a creature half man and half horse is seen here. They are very old in Greek legend, much older than Homer and they appear in both of his epics. In mythology, the centaurs were begotten by Ixion, who abused the hospitality of Zeus by casting lustful eyes on Hera. Zeus divined his intentions and fashioned a false Hera from a cloud. Ixion, too drunk to notice anything wrong, seduced the cloud woman, Nephele, and was then bound by Zeus in punishment to a fiery wheel which rolled across the sky eternally, while Nephele descended to earth and gave birth to a son, Centaurus. This son mated with the mares of Mount Pelion and thus sired the race of centaurs. Generally they were wild, lustful, and strongly attracted to wine. The exception was the wise and kind medicine-man Chiron, who differed from the others being of divine origin.

Plate 67 and 68

Eros was the god of love in Greek mythology, the son of Aphrodite by either Ares or Hermes (there are differing traditions). Homer never mentions Eros as a god, simply referring to *eros* as the force that impels lovers to one another—and makes wise men speak in the language of fools. Hesiod on the other hand believed him to be one of the oldest and most powerful gods, since neither men nor the gods themselves were proof against him. As the personification of physical love he had a large following among the Greeks and he was celebrated annually in a number of festivals. The one in Athens was held in the Spring and phallic symbols have been found in the ruins of his sanctuary. In Greek art he was originally shown as a young man carrying his bow and walking over flowers and plants, as in the gold-painted lekythos. By the Hellenistic period he had become the more familiar baby-like figure, often asleep, as in the marble statue from Paphos.

67

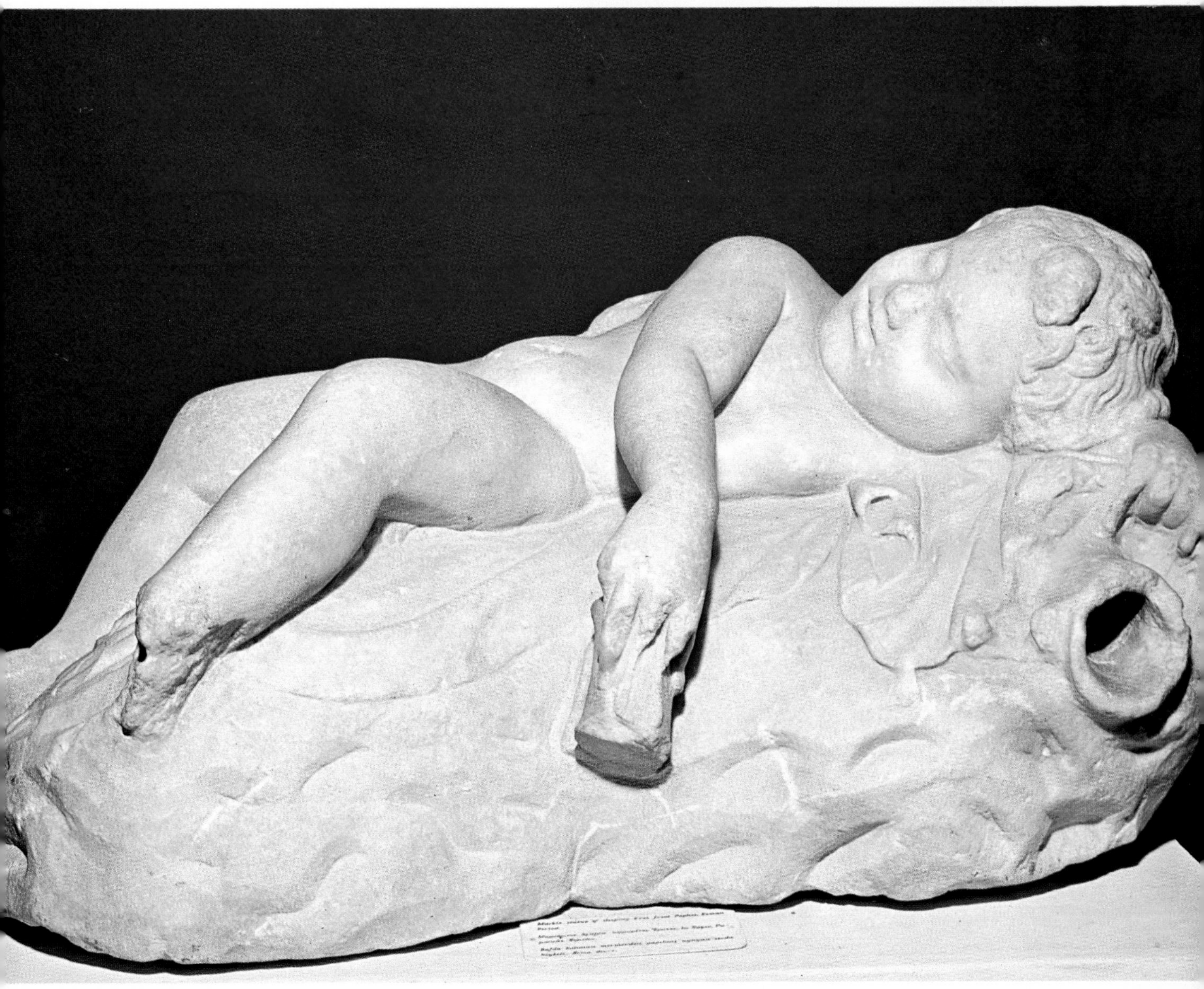

68

69

70

Plate 69

Chiron the centaur with the young Achilles. Chiron played the part of mentor and guardian to Achilles, Jason, Heracles and many other Greek heroes. He was possibly in origin a priest-king of the horse breeders of Thessaly, one to whom they ascribed all wisdom. It was inevitable that his stature increased as the tradition extended down the centuries. Some myths describe him as the king of the centaurs; others say that he was the son of Cronus and therefore immortal. His immortality was to prove no boon; Heracles, while performing his Fourth Labour, accidentally wounded Chiron in the knee—and Heracles used arrows dipped in the poison of Hydra. The wound would have been fatal to a mortal but for Chiron it was infinitely worse, since he would have to endure eternal pain. At length the cruel impasse was overcome; Zeus allowed Chiron to surrender his immortality to Prometheus, and die in peace. Wall painting from Herculaneum.

Plate 70

A view of the Greek countryside with a glimpse of Delphi in the distance. The Greeks acknowledged the spirits of nature in many different ways and the most familiar to us are perhaps the nymphs. Usually believed to be young and beautiful, they were benevolent to mankind as a rule but were not to be trifled with. They punished unresponsive lovers and sometimes stole young men for themselves; they were very like the fairies of later days. There was an infinite variety of them; those of the forests and groves were Dryads, those of meadows Leimoniads, those of mountains Orestiads. There were also the water nymphs; Naiads, Potameids, Creneids and Hydriads. In contrast to the gods the nymphs were mortal, though they were blessed, according to Hesiod, with very long lives.

Plate 71

A Harpy carrying off a child. The Harpies (the name is from a Greek word meaning 'snatchers') were, according to Homer and Hesiod, the personification of violent winds—strong enough to snatch people away. They were usually depicted as birds with the faces of women, and in mythology they are described as the daughters of Thaumas and Electra (daughter of Oceanus—not the sister of Orestes). They make a notable appearance in the story of the Argonauts: when the voyagers reached Salmydessus they found the king, Phineus, in great distress because the Harpies continually plagued him. He had the gift of prophecy, and had earned the wrath of Zeus for using his gift too accurately. The Harpies snatched the food from his table and defiled what they couldn't carry away. The Argonauts rid Phineus of the Harpies, and in turn he gave them valuable advice about the voyage. The relief shown here is in the British Museum and comes from a tomb of the fifth century BC found at Xanthos in Asia Minor.

V
THE STUFF OF TRAGEDY

72

Plate 72

Orpheus and the beasts as depicted on a mosaic from Tarsus of the third century AD. Orpheus is one of the most celebrated figures in Greek mythology—and one of the most difficult to identify. According to the myths surrounding him he was the son of the Muse Calliope, and a musician of such power and sweetness that the wild creatures would gather to listen to him. He sailed with the Argonauts, and his wife was the dryad Eurydice who, fleeing from the attentions of Aristaeus, trod on a serpent and died from its bite. Orpheus went down to Hades and persuaded him to release her; but the lord of the shades made the condition that Orpheus must believe that Eurydice followed him to earth—and not look back. But in his agony of uncertainty that Eurydice was really following him Orpheus did look back, and saw her slip away from him for ever.

Plate 73

. . . and in her husband's absence she took a lover, Aegisthus, and waited for the day when she could be revenged on Agamemnon. When he returned from Troy she gave him a welcome befitting a warrior king; but then murdered both him and Cassandra when they entered the palace. This is one of the strange beehive tombs of Mycenae, which were built into the side of the hill and given their shape by the use of the corbeled vault. This is variously called 'the Treasury of Atreus' and 'the Tomb of Clytemnestra' but the actual use to which the building was put cannot be determined. If it was indeed a tomb for Clytemnestra its strangeness is well suited to the extraordinary woman the Greek tragedians put into their plays. She is a tremendous figure in the *Agamemnon* of Aeschylus; and also appears in the sequel, *The Liberation Bearers.*

73

Plate 74

The Lion Gate, the entrance to the citadel of Mycenae. Agamemnon was king of Mycenae and the leader of the Achaean armies that went to Troy to avenge the stealing of Helen, the most beautiful of all women and the wife of Menelaus, the king of Sparta. The brothers and their Achaean allies were eventually victorious—but the war had dragged on for ten years. Agamemnon, who may well have been an historic personage, might have ridden under the Lion Gate in the chariot that brought him home, apparently in triumph. Also in the chariot would have been Cassandra, the princess of Troy he claimed as part of his spoils. But there had been another princess—Agamemnon's daughter Iphigenia, and he had used her as a sacrifice when the Achaen fleet was held up at Aulis by contrary winds. He tricked his wife Clytemnestra into bringing the girl to Aulis, saying that she was to become the wife of Achilles. Clytemnestra had been waiting ten years for the king to return. . . .

74

Plate 75

A fifth-century terracotta showing Electra and Orestes at the tomb of Agamemnon. The great tragic cycle which begins with the sacrifice of Iphigenia rolls on relentlessly. The most famous dramatic version of the next stage of events is probably the *Electra* of Sophocles but the scene shown here, moving though it is, is not used by that master. It occurs in the *Electra* of Euripides and *The Libation Bearers* of Aeschylus, and deals with the encounter of brother and sister at their father's tomb. In the play by Aeschylus, Orestes has been in exile since the murder of his father. He returns with his friend Pylades and, going at once to his father's tomb, dedicates on it a lock of his hair. The two withdraw upon the approach of Electra and her attendants, who have been sent to pour libations on the tomb by their guilty mother Clytemnestra who has been troubled by ominous dreams. Electra recognizes the lock of hair—exactly like her own—and brother and sister are reunited.

75

76

77

Plate 76

Orestes avenges the death of his father, Agamemnon. Detail from an amphora in the British Museum. After the encounter at the tomb, Orestes and Pylades proceed to the palace in disguise and tell Clytemnestra that Orestes her son is dead. Exultant, the queen sends for her lover Aegisthus, believing that there can be no threat now to their happiness and safety. When Aegisthus arrives Orestes kills him in front of the Queen. She pleads for her life, and Orestes falters; but he has been commanded by Apollo and drags his mother inside the palace and murders her too.

Plate 77

Cadmus, the brother of Europa and the founder of Thebes. The Delphic oracle told him to follow a cow and found a city where the creature first lay down. This he did, then Athene instructed him to sow the teeth of the dragon he had just killed, and from them grew warriors fully armed. Cadmus provoked these to fight each other by throwing a stone amongst them, and the five best fighters who survived became the ancestors of the noble families of Thebes.

Plate 78

The meeting with the Sphinx, an incident in the tragic life of Oedipus, who became king of Thebes. His father Laius had brought a curse on his family and he was warned by Apollo that his own son would kill him. This was Oedipus, and Laius drove a spike through the baby's feet and left him to die on Mount Cithaeron. A shepherd found him and took him to Polybus and Merope, king and queen of Corinth, who brought him up as their son. Later, upset by taunts that he was no true son of Polybus, Oedipus enquired of the Delphic oracle concerning his true parentage. The oracle only told him that he would bring destruction on his father and marry his own mother, and the horrified Oedipus, loving Polybus and Merope as the only parents he knew, fled from Corinth to avoid doing them harm. On his journey he came to a place where three roads met, and there encountered a man in a chariot who ordered him to get out of his way. A fight ensued and Oedipus killed the man in the chariot who was Laius, his real father. Oedipus went on, and defeated the Sphinx that plagued the city of Thebes, and as a result he was welcomed as a hero. He was offered the hand of Jocasta, the widowed queen, and the throne—the oracle was fulfilled. By his wife-mother, Oedipus became the father of two sons and two daughters, and all went well until, in a time of famine and disease, the oracle was to wreak havoc with him again; the city would know peace, it said, when the unknown murderer of Laius was discovered and cast out. Oedipus sets out to find the truth, and when he does it is too awful to bear; Jocasta hangs herself and Oedipus puts out his eyes. He leaves the city, a blinded exile, attended by his daughter Antigone.

VI
THE HEROES

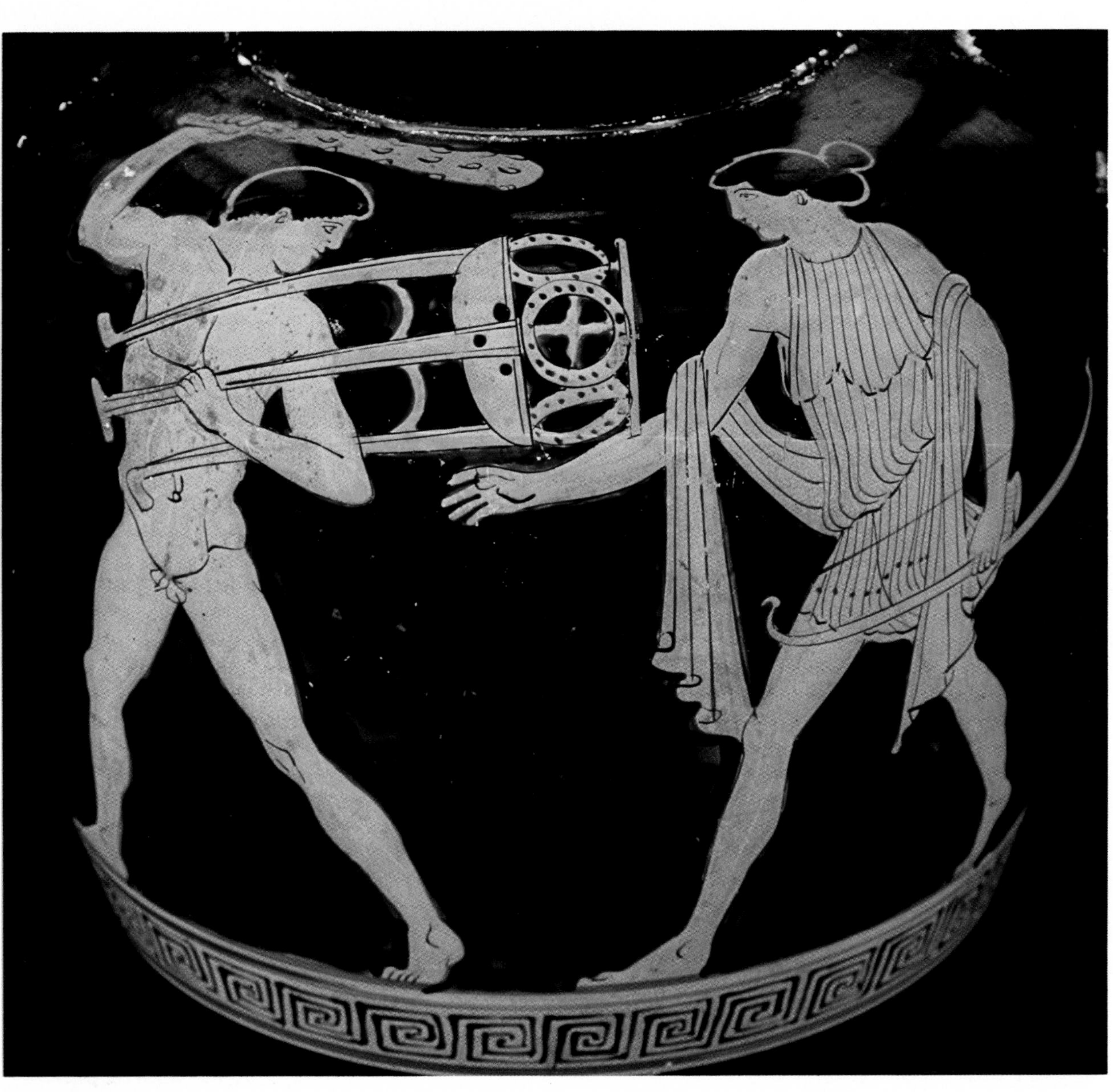

79

Plate 94

Menelaus and Hector, the Trojan prince, in combat. The dead man is the Trojan, Euphorbus, and this painted plate from Rhodes is known as the Euphorbus plate. Patroclus led the attack on Troy while Achilles was sulking in his tent, and Euphorbus gave him his first wound; Hector finished him off. Menelaus killed Euphorbus—but did not long try conclusions with the great Hector. However, he and Ajax returned for the body of Patroclus and bore it back to the Achaean camp. It was this that roused Achilles from his sulks; he loved Patroclus, and the news that he was killed roused Achilles to fury. He meant to have Hector's life in return.

94

Plate 95

Hector and Achilles face to face. Achilles mounted a furious attack on the Trojans that drove them back into the city. Hector met him at the Scaean Gate and the two champions knew that one of them must fall. It was Hector. To the horror of the Trojans watching from the walls, Achilles despoiled the corpse by tying it to the back of his chariot and dragging it through the dust back to his camp. There he sacrified twelve Trojan prisoners on the funeral pyre of Patroclus; but he intended that Hector's body should be thrown to the dogs. In the meantime he went on despoiling it, but Apollo was moved to compassion and preserved his body from damage. On the twelfth day the gods, outraged by Achilles' vile behaviour, decided that Hector's body should be restored to his father Priam for decent burial. The Messenger goddess Iris went to Troy, and inspired Priam to go to the Achaen camp. The old king pleaded with Achilles, and finally yielded his daughter Polyxena as a bride for Achilles as well as Hector's weight in gold. Achilles gave way, and the corpse of the noble Hector was taken back to Troy for burial.

96

97

Plate 96

After the wooden Horse. The Achaeans took the city, and no mercy was shown to the Trojans. Cassandra, Priam's daughter, fled to the temple of Athene for sanctuary. She was pursued there by Ajax who dragged her away from the altar; thus he earned the wrath of Athene and the loathing of the other Achaeans for violating a sacred shrine. The painting of this fourth-century lekythos shows Apollo watching the scene. Apollo had fallen in love with Cassandra but she had resisted him; in consequence the god had given her the gift of prophecy—and then made it useless. No one believed her, though she had in fact prophesied the city's doom. Ajax had to yield Cassandra to Agamemnon when the spoils were divided, and she met the same fate as her captor when he returned to Mycenae.

Plate 97

The sack of Troy. Priam, lying on the ground, was killed by Neoptolemus, the son of Achilles. Hecuba, the queen of Troy, fell to the lot of Odysseus, though this fact was lost in the telling of his subsequent adventures. The son of Hector and Andromache, the last of the Trojan royal line, is seen being carried off by the Achaean herald, Talthybius. The child could not be allowed to live, and Talthybius, acting on the orders of Odysseus, hurled him from the walls. Andromache was given to Neoptolemus, and Polyxena was sacrificed on the tomb of Achilles. The beautiful Helen, the apparent cause of the war, was threatened with death by her husband Menelaus but her beauty destroyed his resolve and he took her back to Sparta with him. The Achaeans destroyed the city by fire after plundering it.

Plate 98

On his way home from Troy Odysseus landed on the island of the Cyclops, giant herdsmen who were said to be the sons of Poseidon, and who had only one eye. Odysseus and his companions explored a cave which proved to be the home of one of the Cyclops, Polyphemus, who returned unexpectedly and sealed the exit with a huge rock after his flock of sheep were safely inside. He discovered the men and promptly ate two of them; the next day he ate two more. Odysseus, in the way of epic heroes, just happened to have a full wine-skin with him, which sent Polyphemus into a drunken sleep. Odysseus took a burning brand from the fire in the cave and thrust it into the giant's single eye; Polyphemus in his agony screamed for his brother Cyclops to come and help him. Now Odysseus, asked by Polyphemus who he was, had answered 'I am Noman'. When his brother Cyclops asked Polyphemus what he was screaming about he told them that Noman had blinded him. They went away again, annoyed that he should be raving about something that no man was doing to him; and assuming he was having nightmares.

99

100

Plate 99

When the dawn came Polyphemus rolled away the rock that sealed the cave, as his flock had to be let out to pasture; but he sat by the entrance and used his hands to tell him which creatures were leaving the cave. Odysseus tied his men under the bellies of the finest rams and in this way they escaped from the Cyclops. There was no one to tie Odysseus so he chose the biggest ram, the leader of the flock, and simply clung to the fleece. This bronze from Delphi shows him making his escape. With the remainder of his men Odysseus got back to his ship and took his rams on board to provide meat for the crew. Then he stood at the prow and shouted taunts at the blinded giant, who responded by hurling huge rocks at the ship. Not being able to see the ship he failed to destroy it; but he called on his father Poseidon to avenge him. Falling foul of the sea god was unwise, as Odysseus was to discover; a journey back from the Trojan war was to last ten years.

Plate 100

An Attic vase painting of the fifth century BC showing Odysseus and the Sirens. When he left the island of Aeaea he was warned by Circe that he would have to sail past the Sirens, who lured the crews of ships to destruction on the rocks by their sweet singing—no one who heard the song could resist following it. (They make an appearance in the epic of the Argonauts also; but on that occasion they could not compete with Orpheus, who outsang them). Odysseus ordered his men to bind him to the mast of the ship, first taking the precaution to block up their ears to prevent them from hearing the songs themselves. In this way the Sirens were safely eluded. They were half woman and half bird, and their conception may have been an echo of the time when birds were regarded as messengers of death. Some traditions said that the Sirens died if their song was resisted, and one of them can be seen falling dead into the sea.

Plate 101

Odysseus and Circe, from a Theban vase of the fourth century. Circe, looking somewhat less than an enchantress, offers a drink to Odysseus, who looks somewhat less than a hero. The events of the Trojan war and the return of Odysseus were favourite subjects among the Greek painters and the quality of the work was, inevitably, of enormous range, and this representation is not one of the best. On the island of Aeaea Odysseus went off to explore, and when he returned to the ship divided his company into two parties to go and investigate the smoke he had seen rising from a clearing. One party found the palace of Circe; she invited them in and gave them food and drink. But the food turned them into pigs. Odysseus, going to their rescue, was warned by the god Hermes, who gave him a magic herb known only to the gods. So Odysseus was immune to Circe's magic, and he forced her to restore his men to their human form. However he was not immune to Circe's personal charms; he dallied with her for a whole year.

101

Plate 102

When Odysseus finally reached Ithaca he disguised himself as a beggar on the advice of the goddess Athene. His first encounter was with his old swineherd Eumaeus, who told the stranger of what had befallen in the palace while the king was away on a war from which he had never returned; that the palace was full of suitors despoiling the king's household, and trying to persuade Penelope, the queen, to marry one of them in the hope of gaining the throne. Odysseus continued to the palace, having made himself known to his son Telemachus, and there was only recognized by his old dog Argus who, lying neglected on a dung heap, was able to give him one last, hopeful wag of his tail before dying. Penelope, hearing from the stranger that he knew her husband, treated him as an honoured guest and asked his old nurse, Eurycleia, to bring water and wash the stranger's feet. The incident is shown here on a Roman relief of the first century AD. Eurycleia recognized Odysseus by an old scar from a wound he had sustained while hunting boar. Eventually Odysseus made himself known to Penelope; but not until he had killed the suitors and regained his kingdom.

102

ACKNOWLEDGMENTS

The publishers would like to thank the following individuals and organizations for their kind permission to reproduce the pictures in this book:

	Page
F H C Birch/Sonia Halliday Photographs	3, 16, 18, 91, 21, 22 top, 28, 29 top, 31, 33 centre and bottom, 35 bottom, 49, 55 top and centre.
BPC Library	24–25.
C M Dixon	17, 20, 22 bottom, 23 (& jacket), 24, 26 top, 27, 29 bottom, 30 top, 38, 39 top, 40 top, 43 centre, 44, 52 bottom, 53, 57, 60 bottom, 62 bottom, 64 top, 70 top, 71 top.
Giraudon (Musé Louvre)	42 bottom, 55 bottom, 63, 65 top.
Sonia Halliday Photographs	33 top, 39 bottom, 40 bottom, 41, 46 top, 48 bottom, 51, 54, 60 top, 61 bottom, 65 bottom.
Andre Held/ Joseph Ziolo	29 centre, 32 top, 34 top.
Hirmer Fotoarchiv	2, 26 bottom, 43 bottom.
Michael Holford	endpapers, 30 bottom, 34 centre and bottom, 36, 37 bottom, 42 top, 43 top, 46 bottom, 48 top and centre, 50 top and centre, 51 top, 56, 58, 59, 61 top, 64 bottom, 66, 67, 68, 69, 70 bottom, 71 bottom.
Roland/Joseph Ziolo	7, 32 bottom.
Scala	22 centre, 52 top.
Spectrum	1, 11, 35 top, 37 top, 38 bottom, 45, 47.